PRINCESS DIANA

A Life from Beginning to End

D0840394

Table of Contents

Introduction

She wasn't born a princess, and her cradle didn't come readily equipped with a royal scepter. Still, the family that Diana Frances Spencer was born into on July 1, 1961, was by no means of low birth. Although she wasn't born royal, her family was considered a part of the British nobility, with a long family tree of knights, barons, and the like. Her grandfather Albert, in fact, was the seventh Earl Spencer. When he later passed, this then made Diana's father John the eighth Earl Spencer. Diana's mother, Frances, was also of noble blood, being the daughter of a baron.

Diana was preceded in birth by a couple of elder sisters—Jane and Sarah. Her mother had also birthed a son, but the infant boy perished shortly after birth. Diana would later relate how when her mother became pregnant shortly after the death of their baby boy, her parents had hoped that the child would be male. When Diana was born, their disappointment was palpable, and they waited a full week before they decided on a name for the baby girl.

Her parents did eventually have another son, a boy they named Charles, ostensibly relieving

Diana of this burden. Nevertheless, Diana would always feel a certain sense of insecurity. Some say that her drive to prove herself and to make her family proud just might stem from the feelings of disappointment that her parents had initially expressed. Little did they know just how far Lady Diana would come.

Chapter One

Early Life as an Earl's Daughter

"I like to be a free spirit. Some don't like that—
but that's the way I am."

—Princess Diana

Diana was a happy-go-lucky child and loved playing with her friends, especially those of the furry and four-footed kind. She is said to have had a love for animals from a young age and had quite a wide variety of critters at her disposal at any given time. There were cats, dogs, rabbits, and even a guinea pig called Peanuts.

It was not all fun and games for young Diana, however, and in 1967, at just six years of age, she would for the first time become acquainted with grief. This grief wasn't over the passing of a loved one but rather over her parents' separation. Diana would always remember what it was like when this rupture occurred. Her older sisters were in boarding school, and it was just her and her little brother Charles at home with their parents. One day, she saw her mother Frances hurriedly gathering her things and simply walking out the door. Diana then heard her mother leave the house, start her car, and drive off.

For the first few weeks, little Diana didn't even know if she would see her mother again, but this was just a mere transition as her parents hammered out the terms of their separation. In a matter of weeks, Diana and Charles were sent to live with their mother, with arrangements made for their father to see them on the weekend. After the following Christmas, however, John had his children return to his home, and by 1969, when the terms of her parents' divorce were finalized, John ended up getting custody of little Diana and her siblings.

One month after the divorce was finalized, Diana's mother married Peter Shand Kydd, the heir to a wallpaper fortune. It's said that Diana's mother had carried on an affair with this man prior to her separation from her husband, and it was the affair that led to the divorce and ultimately to Diana's father getting custody of the children. Frances had met Mr. Kydd in 1966, and she informed her husband of their relationship by the fall of 1967. The separation followed soon thereafter, leading to the fateful finalization of their divorce in 1969.

Diana and her siblings were just innocent bystanders to a drama not of their own making, yet they were deeply affected by it, all the same. Diana certainly wasn't happy with the way things turned out, but she still got to see her mother on the weekends, and as any child might, she tried to make the best of a sad situation.

In the midst of all this, Diana found herself in boarding school. At nine years of age, she was enrolled in the prestigious prep school confines of Riddlesworth Hall. Like many youngsters in her situation, Diana was a bit anxious about the change in her living situation. Her only solace at this time was the fact that she was permitted to bring her pet guinea pig, Peanuts, along for the move. Fortunately, as it turned out, she had nothing at all to worry about; she proved to be quite popular at Riddlesworth, and here she forged plenty of friendships.

Diana would remain at the boarding school for the next four years before she was transferred to another school in 1973 called West Heath. Her grades dipped a bit at West Heath, and she failed some of the standardized tests, having to repeat them later on. Nevertheless, it was at West Heath that Diana would first get involved with what would later become a true calling—doing charitable work for others.

At West Heath, Diana took part in a special aid program sponsored by the school. The program would have her, along with other students, go to a local nursing home for those suffering from both physical and mental conditions. Once there, she and her peers would tend to those interred therein. As she cared for the patients, Diana immediately felt that she had found her niche, and such work would become a big part of her life from there on out.

At age 16, Diana graduated from West Heath. Around the same time, her father decided to marry another woman, a lady by the name of Raine. Diana and her siblings did not like Raine from the beginning, and this feeling seemed to be mutual. Diana later described Raine as nothing but a "bully." In response, she developed a form of chastisement for her stepmother by periodically chanting, "Raine, Raine, go away—come again some other day!" The words were, of course, taken from the children's rhyme of a similar sound.

It was childish, to be sure, but Diana had a lot of built-up frustration at this point over her parents' divorce, and her stepmother Raine often became the focal point of it. She didn't like the circumstances she found herself in, but nevertheless, Diana would have to learn to make do with what life had in store.

Chapter Two

Soothing the Sorrow of a Prince

"I knew what my job was; it was to go out and meet the people and love them."

—Princess Diana

Despite the occasional portrayal of Diana as a commoner, in reality, she had rubbed shoulders with royals from a young age. Her father's home, in fact, is said to have been within walking distance of one of the royal family's favorite vacation homes. From this perch, Diana and her family would occasionally get glimpses of the royals.

Before Diana was introduced to Prince Charles, her older sister Sarah had already met him. It was actually Sarah who arranged Diana's introduction to the prince when, in November of 1977, she invited Diana to a party at which the prince would be in attendance. Diana was 16 years old at the time, whereas the eligible bachelor Charles was already 29. It remains a bit unclear how much of an impression the energetic 16-year-old made on Charles at the time, but later on, he did claim to remember the young girl, remarking that she was "a very jolly, amusing, and attractive 16-year-old, full of fun."

It was shortly after this momentous occasion that Diana was sent off to a so-called finishing school in Switzerland. This type of school was typically dedicated to the refinement of "social graces." The curriculum at this school was presented in French. Diana had studied French in the past, but keeping up with other more fluent French speakers was indeed a challenge. Diana, feeling that she wasn't able to fit in at the school, eventually went back home in the spring of 1978.

Diana was desperately trying to figure out what to do with her life when tragedy struck. In September of that same year, her father John became gravely ill. Seemingly out of nowhere, he was hit with a splitting headache, and shortly thereafter, he passed out. It was after he was taken to the hospital that it would be learned that he had just suffered a brain aneurism.

Aneurisms like this occur when blood vessels burst in the brain and cause blood to leak into the brain. Since the brain is normally separated from the bloodstream by a blood-brain barrier, this is not good, and the effects are severe. As it pertained to Earl Spencer, things looked grim. John's wife Raine, as well as his children, were brought before him as if it were going to be the last time.

As much as the children had previously disapproved of Raine, she became a source of strength at this point, and it was she who mobilized all of the efforts to save John's life. She even went so far as to get John access to an experimental drug, which some believe may have been of great consequence. Whatever the case may be, John did recover, but even so, he was severely weakened from the ordeal and was never quite the same.

Upon his return home, Raine took on an even more domineering role and began to extensively remodel the family home. In order to raise funds, she sold much of Earl Spencer's family heirlooms, something which didn't help endear her with Diana and her siblings.

At any rate, Diana struggled through the often-tumultuous emotional environment of her father and stepmother's home until 1979, when the then 18-year-old Diana decided to move out and live on her own. Packing up her things, the young woman moved to the heart of London, where she would live in a small, tidy apartment, along with a few other young women—Anne Bolton, Virginia Pitman, and Carolyn Pride.

Diana, always enjoying jobs that allowed her to help others, found work at a school teaching kids in kindergarten. Here, she was apparently a hit, and both the parents and the young children appreciated the work that she did. Diana proved to be long-suffering with even the most hyperactive of youngsters and quite good at getting the students to follow her instructions.

Building on this experience, in the spring of 1980, she became an employee of a childcare outsourcing outfit called Occasional Nannies. This agency led her to be hired by a woman from the United States who was in England on business. Mary Robertson charged Diana with the task of looking after her boy Patrick while she was away. Diana is said to have developed an immediate bond with the child, and his mother Mary was quite impressed.

Besides her day job of taking care of children, Diana had a growing nightlife, in which she would attend parties and other social events with locals of similarly wealthy backgrounds. It was during her forays with this well-to-do set that she would once again make the acquaintance of Prince Charles. In July, when she was at a party that he happened to be in attendance, Diana picked up on a hint of sadness from this party-going prince. She inquired with him about his gloomy disposition, and the two then spoke of how the prince's great uncle—Lord Mountbatten—had recently passed.

The passing was not a natural one since the old man had been killed in an attack launched by the IRA (Irish Republican Army). In those days, the IRA was openly hostile to the British government and most especially the royal family. For a young royal like Charles, both the personal loss and the malicious assault on his very identity as a royal were absolutely earth-shattering. Diana immediately seemed to understand the depths of Charles's grief, and as was her way, she helped soothe his sorrow. Soon thereafter, the two would begin their courtship in earnest.

Chapter Three

Marriage to Charles

"They say it is better to be poor and happy than rich and miserable, but how about a compromise like moderately rich and just moody?"

—Princess Diana

Diana and Prince Charles had a whirlwind of a courtship that kicked off in the summer of 1980. Before the year was even out, there was talk of marriage. Prince Charles was in his early thirties by then and had dated several women, so the fact that he had decided upon marriage with Diana so quickly was a clear indication of just how smitten he was with her. To him, she appeared bride material, and not long thereafter, a date was set.

On February 24, 1981, 19-year-old Diana Spencer and 31-year-old Prince Charles were engaged to be married. As soon as the announcement was made, there was an absolute media frenzy, and Prince Charles and Lady Diana could go hardly anywhere without encountering the flashing cameras of photographers. Prince Charles was an avid outdoorsman at the time, and on one occasion, reporters even followed them while they were on a fishing trip. To Diana's utter embarrassment, photographers also began to show up at her workplace. Prince Charles was by now used to this kind of publicity, but for Diana, it was a brand-new experience.

Shortly after the announcement of her engagement to Prince Charles, Diana quit work and moved into the so-called Clarence House, the residence at which the queen of England—Elizabeth II—resided. The idea of living under the same roof with Prince Charles's mother must have been nerve-wracking, but Clarence House was a huge compound, so it wasn't as if they were in close quarters with each other.

As it turned out, the potential tension and intrigue between the bride-to-be and her future mother-in-law was the least that Diana had to worry about. It was around this time that Diana was beginning to realize the closeness of relations between Prince Charles and a certain Camilla Parker Bowles. Mrs. Bowles a woman of some distinction and well-acquainted with the royal family—so well-acquainted, in fact, that it has been said that Prince Charles carried on an affair with her both before and after his marriage to Diana. Such things are a bit too much to get into at this point in our telling of Diana's life, but even back then, Diana was becoming aware of this potential, extra romantic fixture which was seemingly attached to Charles.

Camilla Parker Bowles was friendly enough at first; she even sent Diana a letter of congratulations shortly after her arrival at Clarence House. Diana found the letter carefully placed on her bed. It read in part, "Such exciting news about the engagement. Do let's have lunch soon. I'd love to see the ring." One could credit Mrs. Bowles for the attempt to reach out and befriend young Diana, but shortly after Diana was shuffled off to Buckingham Palace to prepare herself for her impending wedding, this entreaty seems to have fallen flat.

It was soon after her arrival to Buckingham Palace that Diana learned that Charles had ordered flowers to be sent to Camilla. It would be frustrating for any woman—especially a woman getting ready to get married—to learn that her fiancé had sent flowers to another. However, giving Charles a bit of cover at the time was the fact that Camilla had been sick, so the flowers were ostensibly an innocent "get well soon" kind of gift to this royal hanger-on. Regardless of the excuse, eventually such niceties would become harder and harder for Diana to ignore.

At any rate, after much anxious waiting and preparation, the fateful day finally arrived on July 29, 1981. This wedding would, of course, be a major affair in which the entire British public would be involved in the seeing off of their favorite son, Prince Charles. Yet as much as the public had long been enamored with Charles, it was 20-year-old Diana who stole the show. Like something out of a fairy tale, she arrived at St. Paul's Cathedral, the site of her wedding, in a glass coach. Diana pulled up in her see-through carriage and waved to the delighted crowd of 600,000 people that had gathered around. Not only was there a large number of people watching in person, but the event was also televised all over the world to an audience of some 750 million people.

Diana was an instant celebrity simply for getting married. Her marriage into an ancient royal family was considered a huge deal and was marketed as such. The TV network NBC even dubbed the event "The Wedding of the Century." As such, all eyes were on Diana as she made her way to the altar, with what seemed like a mile-long train of a dress following behind her. Prince Charles, decked out in full royal regalia, was standing there, calmly waiting for her. The two were then married with much fanfare before heading off to a special wedding breakfast, where the celebration would continue.

It was only after this fanfare had subsided that Prince Charles and the newly christened Princess Diana were able to depart for their honeymoon. They took a plane to Gibraltar before hopping on a yacht to sail the seas. The yacht itself was huge, yet besides the ship's officers, deckhands, and other employees onboard the craft, Diana and Charles had it practically to themselves. Even so, there was a constant intrusion of glitz and glamour even on the yacht. Simply eating dinner on the deck was always accompanied by a full-blown Royal Marine band.

Diana also learned that she was not exactly free to do what she wanted and, at times, would experience friction with expected royal protocol. By the time the honeymoon was over, there was already talk of Princess Diana being unhappy with her lot in life. It became so bad that fall that Prince Charles convinced Princess Diana to talk to a therapist. During these early therapy sessions, Princess Diana admitted to her counselor that she was indeed having trouble adjusting to the royal life. She was prescribed Valium to help soothe her nerves, but Diana refused to take it. Charles was equally aghast and agreed with his wife that she shouldn't start a regimen of such a powerful medication.

In the meantime, Diana found out she was pregnant, and this news would greatly change her disposition. Over the next several months, she became an excited, expectant mother. Even so, the couple continued to have arguments from time to time, and on one occasion, the arguing was said to have been particularly bad. Although some of Diana's friends later denied it, there is an account of her becoming so frustrated and despondent that she threw herself down a flight of stairs. Charles was apparently getting ready to go out with his friends, but Diana did not want him to leave. It was then that Diana supposedly hurled herself down the staircase, pregnant belly and all.

Even so, when her firstborn son, Prince William, was born on June 21, 1982, her troubles seemed to be behind her, at least for the time being.

Chapter Four

Princes William and Harry

"Being a princess isn't all it's cracked up to be."

—Princess Diana

Shortly after the birth of their first child, Diana and Charles embarked upon a tour of Australia and New Zealand. Many might have suggested that she take a break, but Diana was ready for some adventure, and she brought her newborn son along for the ride. The decision proved to be popular with the Australian masses, as spectators vied to have a closer look at the newest royal.

Shortly after their tour of Australia and New Zealand came to a close, Diana, Charles, and William made their way to Canada, where they encountered droves of adoring well-wishers. Diana managed to celebrate her 22nd birthday while on Canadian soil on July 1, 1983. On that particular day—which just so happened to coincide with that year's Canada Day—she was serenaded by a stadium full of Canadian admirers who sang "Happy Birthday" just for her. The couple was in attendance at Canada's Edmonton Stadium, taking in the festive atmosphere, when Charles announced to the crowd that Canada Day just so happened to be his wife's birthday. Without fail, the gleeful crowd belted out a rendition of the birthday tune for the princess.

At this point, Diana and Charles seemed to have made up much of their differences and appeared to be genuinely affectionate with each other. The birth of their baby William especially seemed to have strengthened their bond, and the young family very much enjoyed the extravaganza of this outing together. It was shortly after this fateful trip that William's little brother Harry must have been conceived since he was born the following year, on September 15, 1984.

Princess Diana would later relate that it was during her pregnancy with Harry that her and Prince Charles's relationship was the happiest. Strangely enough, as happy as Charles and Diana were during her pregnancy with Harry, she would later claim that it was right after Harry was born that Charles grew increasingly distant. Soon, he was back to his old habit of staying out late with friends, and it was one friend in particular that Diana became increasingly suspicious of. That friend was Charles's old flame, Camilla Parker Bowles.

Charles had promised that he had ended his previous romantic relationship with Camilla, but Diana wasn't buying it. She began to suspect that he was spending his long absences from the home with Camilla. Still, life would go on, and despite her suspicions, Princess Diana, the public figure, had to go on too. Big things were in store.

The following year, Princess Diana and Prince Charles toured Italy and even met with Pope John Paul II. After this visit, they then made another stop in Australia. Yet the trip that brought them the most fanfare by far was their visit to the United States that fall. Their main mission in Washington, D.C. was to visit a new art exhibit called the Treasure Houses of Britain. In the meantime, though, they were invited to the White House to meet up with then-president Ronald Reagan and his wife, Nancy.

This set the stage for an official White House Ball, in which several notable figures were in attendance. The attendees ranged from high-profile political figures to Hollywood celebrities, with the latter providing the most notable exchange when actor and skilled dancer John Travolta managed to secure a dance with the princess. It was memorable enough that Prince Charles himself was later asked about the dance by a reporter, at which the prince—growing increasingly frustrated by all of the attention being lavished on his wife—abruptly quipped that he was "not a glove puppet." He then suggested that they ask Princess Diana about it.

By the time they returned to Britain, the couple was once again at odds with each other, and their lovers' spats quickly evolved into bitter bickering. It was in the midst of this toxic backdrop that both Charles and Diana are said to have engaged in extramarital affairs—Prince Charles with his old flame Camilla and Princess Diana with a major by the name of James Hewitt. Major Hewitt was a part of the palace security detail, an officer of the so-called Life Guards. He was in his late twenties at the time and cut a quite dashing figure.

Diana's relationship with Hewitt is said to have begun around the time that Charles's brother Prince Andrew married Sarah Ferguson, or as she was otherwise known, "Fergie." Fergie was close in age with Diana and quickly became one of her best confidants. As a consequence, Fergie would come to know much about Diana and Charles's extramarital affairs, as well as all the other pertinent details of their continuing spiral toward complete marital collapse. At this point in her life, Diana found Charles too dry and serious, and in Fergie, she had found a true kindred spirit. As lonely as she may have felt in the past, Diana was now carefully cultivating her own group of allies at Buckingham Palace.

Chapter Five

Scandals: Squidgygate

"I think like any marriage, especially when you've had divorced parents like myself, you want to try even harder to make it work."

—Princess Diana

It was sometime in the summer of 1986 that Major James Hewitt was in attendance at a party at Buckingham Palace. It was just one of many such occasions, but this one stood out since it is said to have been the moment when Hewitt and Princess Diana really began to connect.

Diana chatted up Hewitt at this engagement and learned that he was a riding instructor. Princess Diana, who always had a lifelong love of horses, remarked that she would like to have some lessons. With riding lessons as their excuse to be together, it was from here on out that the affair between the two would begin. The lessons took place a few times a week, and along with learning how to ride a horse, the two made time for great conversation, speaking about everything under the sun together.

Diana found a willing listener in Hewitt that she often could not find in her husband Charles. As their dialogue built, soon Diana was inviting Hewitt over for dinner at Kensington Palace, where he would spend the night before quietly slipping away early in the morning. It seems a bit incredible that this relationship would be able to carry on without anyone noticing, but Hewitt and Diana were very careful to find moments alone together without attracting undue attention.

At any rate, by 1987, most had picked up on a decided cooling between Charles and Diana, and increasingly, their public appearances were separate. Nevertheless, Diana was a force to be reckoned with. It was around this time that she began to present herself as a champion for the unfolding AIDS crisis, appearing at special functions to spread awareness of the fight against the illness.

In those days, little was known about AIDS, and many had irrational fears about the disease. Diana did much to ease those fears and let people know that it was completely safe to be around AIDS patients, as the disease is only transferable by exchanging bodily fluids. Back in the 1980s, many were fearful just to be in the room with an AIDS patient, and Diana worked to eliminate this fear by educating the public about the illness.

Her lectures about AIDS were nothing compared to how she led by example, because it was the example of her visits, up close and personal with AIDS patients, shaking their hands and giving them hugs, that proved the most convincing. For those fearful of interacting with people with AIDS, the imagery of Princess Diana fearlessly spending time with them did indeed do wonders to ease those concerns that many people had during the late 1980s and early 1990s.

Probably Diana's best work for AIDS patients then came in 1989 when she saw to the opening of a treatment facility in London called Landmark Aids Centre. The following year, she opened a similar treatment facility in Washington, D.C. called Grandma's House.

In the midst of this flurry of charitable work, the press couldn't help but wonder about the state of Princess Diana's marriage to Prince Charles. They were seen with each other less and less in public, and when they were witnessed together, they seemed decidedly cold to one another— almost as if they were playing a part, and one that they didn't really care for, at that.

Faced with this cool but calm facade, the press naturally wondered what was going on with the royal couple. In January of 1990, they would find out, thanks to a snoop by the name of Cyril Reenan, who managed to eavesdrop on royal phone calls. Both Diana and Charles frequently used early model cell phones, and in those early days of cellular phone use, the calls weren't very secure. Ham radio operators had, in fact, learned how to use special equipment to pick certain calls out of the air. In January of 1990, this is exactly what Cyril Reenan did. After realizing that he was listening in on Princess Diana, he began to record the conversations. Cyril then sent over these taped bits of audio to a tabloid-styled newspaper called *The Sun*.

The voice on the recordings was unmistakably Diana, and the details revealed were scandalous. In the calls, she was frequently speaking to someone by the name of James. This man spoke to her in endearing terms, frequently using words such as "honey" and "darling." He also seemed to have a pet name for Diana—calling her "Squidgy."

Initially, it was assumed that the man on the other end of the phone was none other than James Hewitt. There were indeed already rumors about the closeness between Diana and her riding instructor. This theory was dispelled, however, when in some of the recordings, Diana began to speak of Hewitt to this other James character. It took some detective work, but the people down at *The Sun* managed to figure out that the person that Diana was likely speaking to was a man by the name of James Gilbey.

Some reporters from *The Sun* then tried to interview Gilbey, approaching him and letting him know what they had found out. The startled Gilbey then ran off and informed Diana of what had transpired. Interestingly enough, the people down at *The Sun* showed some restraint and refrained from publishing the explosive story immediately. They apparently had enough respect for the institution of the royal family to delay the release of the bombshell material they had on Princess Diana until further notice. Princess Diana, in the meantime, was left waiting for the other shoe to drop, never knowing when the story might break.

Nevertheless, she made sure that she cultivated good public relations so that the sympathy of the British people would be on her side should the scandal of the tapes leak. By the time *The Sun* finally decided to publish what it knew about these taped conversations in the fall of 1992, Diana was already prepared for the blowback, and by December of that year, the separation of Prince Charles and Princess Diana was already in the works.

Chapter Six

Separation from Prince Charles

"The kindness and affection from the public have carried me through some of the most difficult periods, and always your love and affection have eased the journey."

—Princess Diana

As the year 1992 came to a close, it proved to be a hard one for the entire royal family. Their personal lives seemed as if they were going up in flames, and on November 20, Windsor Castle quite literally caught on fire. The inferno apparently erupted inside Queen Victoria's Private Chapel and then rapidly engulfed its surroundings. By the time the blaze was put out, the royals were looking at millions of pounds in damages.

Just a few days later, on November 24, Queen Elizabeth II gave a speech in which she remarked that "1992 is not a year on which I shall look back with undiluted pleasure." She was ostensibly referring to the recent fire, but she could have just as easily been referring to the incessant drama between Prince Charles and Princess Diana. It was actually the very next day that Charles informed Diana of his desire for a legal separation. With the monarchy being the supposedly transparent, see-through institution that it is, this development was then officially proclaimed on December 9 before the British House of Commons. The whole world now knew that the fairy tale of Prince Charles and Princess Diana was officially coming to an end.

As one might expect, Princess Diana would not spend that December's Christmas with the royal family. Instead, she went on a skiing trip in snowy Colorado in the United States with her good friend Jenni Rivett. Ms. Rivett worked as a fitness trainer, and along with keeping Diana in shape, she was always good at cheering her up. Diana could certainly use it. Along with the fire and the separation, Diana's father had passed away the previous March.

After such a year of turbulence, Diana needed a moment both to reflect and release the pent-up angst she felt. Riding down the ski slopes with

Jenni Rivett proved to be a perfect way to do that. Here, away from the prying eyes of British paparazzi, Diana could relax and enjoy the wind in her hair as she barreled down the snow-laden hills. She would always remember this excursion with particular delight.

At any rate, after the new year of 1993 rolled around, Diana was back to her charitable work and activism. That March, she spoke at a women's shelter called the Chiswick Family Refuge. Here, she spoke before a crowd of women seeking their independence from troubling situations as if she was one who could fully relate.

That same month, Diana made a trip to Nepal accompanied by the Minister for Overseas Development. She wasn't there as part of a national mission but in her own capacity as an individual citizen. She was no longer heralded with the fanfare that she received during official royal engagements, but she was always well-received all the same. No matter what she did, the public remained fascinated with Princess Diana, and even mundane outings, such as taking the young Princes William and Harry to an arcade to play videogames, became a major event.

It was perhaps her relationship with her sons that became the most difficult after her split with Charles. During this period, Diana would voice feelings of persecution, stating that she felt that the rest of the royal family just wished for her to be quiet and disappear so that they could take over the rearing of the young princes themselves. Nevertheless, Diana tried her best to be a normal mother for her two boys. With the paparazzi following her every move, this would be easier said than done.

Diana always tried to ignore the press for the most part, but in the fall of 1993, their intrusiveness would reach new extremes, for it was around that time that suggestive pictures of Diana stretching in a leotard would make the pages of the *Daily Mirror*. As it turned out, a hidden camera had been installed in the ceiling of a gym Diana worked out at. Diana was used to a lot of dirty tricks being played by the paparazzi, but this gross invasion of her privacy was too much to bear. Diana filed a lawsuit against the paper that published the pictures, and as a kneejerk reaction, she stepped back temporarily from public life.

On December 3 of that year, speaking before an organization dedicated to the treatment of spinal cord injuries called Headway, she announced her intentions to take a break from her public appearances. She asked for "time and space" to reflect on what it was that she really wanted to do with her life. It was a decision most of her charitable partners respected, but it still came as a terrific shock. Many of them were used to having Princess Diana represent them as their public face, and it would take some effort for them to adjust. Even so, for business or pleasure, the flash of a camera would never be too far away.

Chapter Seven

Diana Tells All

"I want to walk into a room, be it a hospital for the dying or a hospital for sick children, and feel that I am needed. I want to do, not just to be."

—Princess Diana

After ringing in the new year of 1994, Princess Diana's retreat from the limelight seemed to have been a failure. Even though she had ceased to attend so many charitable functions, the paparazzi continued to follow her no matter where she went. Soon, she was even confronting them, asking them why they hounded her so much. She never got much of a response—just more flashes of the camera.

During one particularly poignant episode, she was caught in traffic, seated in a taxi with camera flashes going off in every direction. Not knowing what else to do, a sad and defeated Diana simply put her head down in her lap in a feeble attempt to hide. Soon, she realized that if she had to face the camera, it might as well be for a good cause. As such, that summer, she came out of her shell and joined up with the Red Cross. Her partnership with the Red Cross had her attending board meetings for the organization in Geneva, Switzerland. She would ultimately leave this outfit by the following fall, however, and would find herself drifting aimlessly in search of meaning and fulfillment once again.

Her two boys—Prince William and Prince Harry—were now in boarding school. Their absence only seemed to magnify the empty void that Diana often felt. Still, she wouldn't stay on the sidelines for long. The following spring, Princess Diana made a trip to Japan, where she met up with none other than the Japanese Emperor Akihito and his wife, Empress Michiko. Diana is said to have been both excited and anxious about the meeting. Always eager to impress, she studiously brushed up on the Japanese language and culture beforehand. Yet the real highlight of her visit came when she visited a children's hospital in Tokyo. As always, Diana's compassion and caring nature were on full display.

After her stint in Japan had come to a close, she then went on over to Hong Kong, which at that time was a British colony. As much of a hit as she was in Japan, she was even more popular in Hong Kong, where she managed to raise considerable sums of money for charitable organizations located therein. As noble as her cause may have seemed, the rest of the royal family did not always approve of these solo missions of goodwill. They were concerned that her trips abroad might have unintended consequences on official British policy.

Diana, for her part, enjoyed her ability to fly solo whenever she chose to do so. Nevertheless, the romantic side of her yearned for a partner, an anchor of emotional stability that she could rely upon when she wasn't gallivanting all over the globe. That very year, she thought she had found the emotional rock she was looking for when she made the acquaintance of a man named Dr. Hasnat Khan, or as Diana called him, "Mr. Wonderful." Khan was a heart surgeon whom Diana had met in the fall of 1995 through a mutual acquaintance.

For Diana, it appears that she fell in love with Hasnat Khan at first sight, and immediately after meeting him, she found every excuse she could to stop by the hospital where he worked. Since she often helped patients as a part of her general charity work, it provided an excellent cover for these early encounters with Dr. Khan. When she was cornered by photographers at the hospital, that was precisely the story she gave them—that she was merely seeking to cheer up the patients. This wasn't a complete lie—she was ostensibly wishing to be of help with the patients—but it left out her primary drive for returning to this particular facility, which was the fact that Dr. Khan happened to work there.

Diana was, at this time, attempting to cultivate better relations with the press. Tired of being ambushed by them, she decided on a more proactive strategy, in which she would come to them to tell her own story. She did so by setting up a primetime interview with BBC newsman Martin Bashir for the television program called *Panorama*. In the initial talks about doing the program, Bashir struck up a strong rapport with Diana and convinced her that he was someone she could trust and one who would help her give a fair presentation of her life and her points of view.

Princess Diana did this knowing that the final terms of her pending divorce from Prince Charles were about to be hammered out. As such, she wanted to present herself in the best possible way so that she could come out on top in the aftermath of what would inevitably be a drama-filled series of events. It was these efforts that would produce a bombshell, tell-all interview, which aired on November 20, 1995.

It's said that some 23 million people in Great Britain alone tuned in to watch Martin Bashir's interview with Princess Diana. In this exclusive interview, Diana candidly spoke about her life: her marriage to Charles, her extramarital affairs, her eating disorders, and her endless struggle with the press.

The royal family, for their part, was understandably stunned by these candid admissions, but what bothered them more than anything was what seemed like an insult hurled directly at Prince Charles when Diana suggested that he might not be a good king. She expressed her skepticism of Prince Charles's ability to rule, even suggesting that he should be skipped in the royal line of succession, with the throne being given directly to Prince William upon Queen Elizabeth's passing.

Princess Diana's words about her scandalous past with James Hewitt also picked up steam, and following the airing of this particularly dirty bit of laundry, the papers were all suddenly speculating about the details of Diana's admitted affair with Hewitt. Still, as damaging as the interview was to the royal family, Diana's efforts did indeed win her some supporters. During the interview with Martin Bashir, she was able to portray herself in a very unique fashion, both as a victim and as a strong and courageous woman who dared to stand up to the monarchy. As such, among her supporters, she was able to generate much sympathy as well as admiration in light of her revelations of what life was like for her at Buckingham Palace.

Shortly after this bombshell report came out, Diana headed off to New York to an award ceremony held in her honor for her work with cerebral palsy patients. As soon as she got back to England, though, Diana would feel the full aftermath of her interview with Bashir. It was shortly after she stepped back on British soil that she was notified that the Queen of England herself was requesting her to officially divorce Prince Charles. The revelations of the *Panorama* interview had been too much to take, and the royal family was hoping to distance themselves from Diana as quickly as they possibly could.

Chapter Eight

After the Divorce

"The biggest disease this day and age is that of people feeling unloved."

—Princess Diana

Although Diana had been looking for a way out of her marriage with Charles for quite some time, she found herself reluctant to do so on command. It seemed that as soon as Queen Elizabeth demanded her exit, she felt like pushing back a bit. Diana was not a lady who liked to be told what to do—even by the Queen of England herself.

When she first became privy to Queen Elizabeth's pressure campaign to have her removed from the family, she initially resisted it and did not immediately reply to the Queen's entreaties. It wasn't until February of 1996 that she finally reached out and came up with the idea that she and Charles should meet alone at St.

James's Palace in order to discuss the final terms of their marital dissolution.

It was at this meeting that Princess Diana informed Prince Charles that she would like to go forward with the divorce but under her conditions. These conditions included a provision that she would be able to remain at Kensington Palace and would also be able to keep an office at St. James's Palace. She also wished to have joint custody of William and Harry, and finally, she wanted to retain the title of princess.

For a woman who sometimes claimed she didn't want to be a royal, the idea that she would refuse to renounce her royal title was quite telling. Nevertheless, Charles obliged her on all of these points, and Princess Diana soon put forward a public statement in which she declared that she and Charles had come to a mutual agreement on their terms of official divorce from each other.

Diana, in the meantime, began her relationship with Dr. Hasnat Khan in earnest. Throughout much of the rest of 1996, the pair were regulars at various London hot spots together. It wasn't long before the news outlets began following her movements. In order to shake off the paparazzi, Diana started to change her appearance, wearing dark sunglasses, headscarves, and at times even wigs.

Along with catching up on London's nightlife, Diana also began spending time at the residence of Khan's British-based relatives. Perhaps the quiet home life that Dr. Khan's extended relatives provided was more attractive than anything else Diana had experienced so far. She often spoke in glowing terms of his loving relatives, who cooked her food and did everything they could to make her feel at home.

Diana also continued to see Khan at the hospital, where she came to admire and respect his dedication to his patients. Diana's presence at the hospital was bound to cause a stir, however, and in April of 1996, when the media got wind that she was standing in to observe Khan perform an operation, it became an absolute circus. Dr. Khan, for one, was beginning to realize that if he were to continue his relationship with Diana, he would have to figure out what it was like to live in the permanently fixed eye of a veritable media storm.

Nevertheless, he and Diana remained close throughout the year, and she even went back with him to his native Pakistan on at least two separate occasions. It was here that she met Khan's mom,

Naheed, and made attempts to convince her that she would make for a good spouse for her son. Despite all of Princess Diana's charm, glitz, and glamour, though, Naheed was not quite so convinced. Like her son, she realized that life in the public eye would be difficult.

The wider world, in the meantime, was beginning to catch on to the relationship, and in November of 1996, a British tabloid called the *Sunday Mirror* did a piece on the couple. Diana was, at this point, ready to let the world know about the man she loved, but some of her friends were a little worried that she was taking things just a bit too fast.

Chapter Nine

Late Life and Charitable Work

"I don't want expensive gifts; I don't want to be bought. I have everything I want. I just want someone to be there for me, to make me feel safe and secure."

—Princess Diana

Diana stepped up her charitable work considerably in 1997. Most notably, her work with the HALO Trust—a group dedicated to removing landmines—gained attention when she went to the African nation of Angola to spread awareness of the minefields that had long been left in that country. She boarded a plane at Heathrow Airport in January of that year, with a long stream of reporters following her every step.

After a brief stopover in Brussels, Princess Diana then ended up in Luanda—the capital city of Angola. After getting off the plane, she was once again met by several reporters on the ground. Diana then gave a brief speech before retiring to her hotel room. Shortly thereafter, Diana went on a wide-ranging tour of Angola, where she saw firsthand the devastation of war. She saw children playing in rubble and people with their limbs blown right off.

On one particularly moving occasion, Diana toured a hospital and greeted those who were grievously injured. Among them was a little girl who had stepped on a landmine and had sustained life-threatening wounds. She was not expected to last much longer. Still, she found the strength to ask an interpreter if perhaps Diana was "an angel." The interpreter struggled to explain that Diana was a princess rather than an angel because, in the minds of many that day, Diana no doubt was an angel. Diana could certainly be combative and even vindictive to those who rubbed her the wrong way, but it was here among those not long for this world that she truly showed that she had a heart of gold.

Yet as much goodwill as she was trying to muster for the cause of Angola, she once again received pushback in Britain. The royal family and others of the elite British establishment began to speak of Diana as a "loose cannon" whose rogue diplomacy was too unpredictable to be tolerated. No one in the British government had authorized her trip to go to Angola, and many in charge did not appreciate her unilateral international efforts.

Shortly after her return, though, sentiments began to change. In May of 1997, the conservative party, which had been previously controlling the British Parliament, was voted out of power in favor of a more liberal one. It was the liberals who took a second look at the problem of mines in places like Angola and generally became more receptive to activist causes such as those that Diana espoused.

Yet as much success as she seemed to have in her professional life, around this time her personal relations with Hasnat Khan had seemingly hit a dead end. His family, it turned out, wasn't all that enthralled by Diana after all, and Dr. Hasnat Khan, a man who wished to abide by his family's wishes, began to distance himself from Diana. Khan would later insist that the reason for his eventual parting from Diana was simply because he realized that he would not be able to deal with her hectic life of fending off the paparazzi on a long-term basis.

Diana initially tried to win Khan back, but after she was seen leaving nightclubs with other men, Khan became even more resolute and began to refuse her phone calls. For all intents and purposes, he was done with the princess. It was shortly thereafter that he would receive the dreadful news that his former lover—Princess Diana—was dead.

Chapter Ten

The Deadly Car Accident

"I'm aware that people I have loved and have died—and are in the spirit world looking after me."

—Princess Diana

It was on August 31, 1997, that reports first began to come in that Princess Diana had perished in a tragic car accident while visiting Paris, France. She had been in the company of a man by the name of Dodi Fayed, enjoying a bit of nightlife when, like usual, the paparazzi pounced. Fed up with the attention and eager to get away, Diana and Dodi hopped into a car and had a man by the name of Henri Paul drive them away from the scene.

Mr. Paul had to drive fast to get away from the pursuing paparazzi, and it seems he drove just a little too fast. While traversing the sometimes-treacherous Pont de l'Alma tunnel, he lost control of the vehicle. The car crashed into the wall of the tunnel on the right side, then careened violently to the left before slamming like a missile into one of the mammoth support pillars for the tunnel. The disabled, mangled car then bounced back like a boomerang before finally coming to a rest against the tunnel wall. Diana, Dodi, and the driver would all die from the impact.

Sickeningly enough, the paparazzi who had been pursuing them were right there at the crash—not rendering aid but snapping photographs. Due to the sheer callousness of these reporters, it was initially widely believed that the paparazzi must have been somehow culpable in causing the vehicle to lose control. Although this aspect of the accident is still argued, it was later revealed that the driver—Henri Paul—was drunk at the time. The fact that their driver had been drinking would most certainly lend credence to the idea that the man simply was driving too fast and, in his inebriated condition, lost control of the vehicle. This was also what an official inquest carried out by Great Britain came up with.

Over a decade later, the whole incident was officially ruled as negligence on the part of the driver, Henri Paul. If this version of events is to be believed, it still does not vindicate the viciousness of these paparazzi, who rushed over to snap photos of this tragic accident. The police did manage to arrive a few minutes later and even put a few of these paparazzi in handcuffs.

The only survivor of the ordeal was a man named Trevor Rees-Jones, who served as a personal bodyguard for Dodi Fayed and the Princess. As for Diana, she was alive for a few hours after the initial impact and was distinctly heard muttering the words, "Oh my God" and "Leave me alone." Diana drifted in and out of consciousness as emergency responders cut her out of the mangled vehicle. She was taken to the hospital in critical condition but would sadly perish from the injuries that she had sustained. The doctors are said to have done everything they could to revive her. They gave her an injection of adrenaline and even a procedure known as a heart massage, which entails a doctor massaging the heart with their own hands. None of it was enough to keep Diana's heart beating, and around 4 am on August 31, Diana would be pronounced dead.

As soon as he was notified, Prince Charles himself would come rushing to his former wife's side. Even after all they had been through, he had never lost his sense of duty to her. He impressed her French attendants with both his own impeccable ability to speak the French language, as well as his professional demeanor. He was a man of action and was ready to set Princess Diane's final affairs in order. He was initially stoic and reserved about the matter, but after viewing what remained of Diana, he was a noticeably changed man. Unable to contain himself, he became utterly distraught, with tears for what had been, as well as perhaps, tears for what might have been seen streaming down his face.

Prince Charles, just like the rest of the world, would soon realize that the fairy tale life he once shared with Princess Diana had finally, and irrevocably, reached its end.

Conclusion

Funerals are always sad occasions, but it could be said that Princess Diana's funeral was indeed a particularly sad affair. On that gloomy day of September 6, 1997, throngs of admirers gathered to grieve. There were multitudes of absolute strangers who somehow felt touched by Diana, yet their sadness was nothing compared to that of Diana's own sons.

It was Prince William and Prince Harry, aged 15 and 12, who had been largely shielded from the glare of the media, who now took center stage in the public consciousness. It's sad for anyone to lose a parent at any age, but given how young and impressionable William and Harry were at the time, coupled with the pressures that being royalty commands, the strain was enormous. Here it was, on display, for the whole world to see. As the procession commenced, these children were openly weeping for their mother.

Diana was indeed a woman that the world thought they knew so well, yet they knew next to nothing when compared to the knowing tears of her children who stood witness to her passing. Prince William and Prince Harry would later reflect on not only their sadness that day but the sadness that they would shoulder for the rest of their lives. In their mother's end, they saw the worst that public life could bring.

Princess Diana's time on this Earth was cut too short, and the short time she was here was often plagued with tumult and turmoil. During the funeral, Elton John sang of Diana's life as if it were a candle in the wind—brilliantly lit for all the world to behold before the tempest around her snuffed it out. Nevertheless, her charm and warmth managed to touch millions. She always put on a brave face and worked her way through her own pain so that she could help others. Princess Diana was many things to many people, but her number one role as comforter-in-chief was indeed best understood by her two boys, William and Harry, and they would cherish her memory forever.

Bibliography

Bradford, Sarah (2006). *Diana.*

Brown, Tina (2007). *The Diana Chronicles.*

Clayton, Tim (2001). *Diana: Story of a Princess.*

Morton, Andrew (2004). *Diana: In Pursuit of Love.*

Morton, Andrew (1997). *Diana: Her True Story – In Her Own Words.*

Simmons, Simone & Seward, Ingrid (2005). *Diana: The Last Word.*

Smith, Sally Bedell (2000). *Diana in Search of Herself: Portrait of a Troubled Princess.*

Made in United States
North Haven, CT
25 June 2022

20612860R00033